THE CREATION

Activity Book for Beginners

The Creation Activity Book for Beginners

Bible Pathway Adventures® is a trademark of BPA Publishing Ltd.

ISBN: 978-1-7772168-9-4

Author: Pip Reid

Creative Director: Curtis Reid

For free Bible resources including coloring pages, worksheets, puzzles and more, visit our website at:

www.biblepathwayadventures.com

Introduction for Parents

Enjoy teaching your children about the Bible with *The Creation Activity Book for Beginners*. Packed with lesson plans, worksheets, coloring pages, and puzzles to help educators just like you teach children a Biblical faith. Includes scripture references for easy Bible verse look-up and a handy answer key for teachers.

Bible Pathway Adventures helps educators teach children a Biblical faith in a fun and creative way. We do this via our Activity Books and free printable activities – available on our website: www.biblepathwayadventures.com

Thanks for buying this Activity Book and supporting our ministry. Every book purchased helps us continue our work providing free Classroom Packs and discipleship resources to families and missions around the world.

The search for Truth is more fun than Tradition!

Table of Contents

LESSON 1 | Lesson Plan
Day & night, water & sky

Teacher: _____

Today's Bible passage: Genesis 1:1-10

Welcome prayer:
Pray a simple prayer with the children before you begin the lesson.

Lesson objectives:
In this lesson, children will learn:
1. What God made on the first day
2. What God made on the second day

Did You Know?
The Bible has many names for God, including Yahweh, Elohim, Yah, Adonai, and Yahuah.

Bible lesson overview:
In the beginning, the earth was empty. God's Spirit moved over the water, and He said, "Let there be light!" The light began to shine. He named the light "day," and the dark "night." There was evening and then there was morning. This was the first day. Then God said, "Let there be a space to separate the water into two parts." Some of the water was above the space and some of the water was below it. God named the space "sky." There was evening, and then there was morning. This was the second day.

Let's Review:

Questions to ask your students:

1. What did God create?
2. What did God name the light?
3. What did God name the dark?
4. How many parts did God separate the water into?
5. What did God name the space between the waters?

 A memory verse to help children remember God's Word:

"God created the heavens and the earth." (Genesis 1:1)

Activities:

Worksheet: Trace the Words
Numbers worksheet: Day one
Numbers worksheet: Day two
Worksheet: Match the pictures
Worksheet: Day and night
Bible craft: Water and sky
Bible craft: Make a rain cloud
Worksheet: Day one
Worksheet: Day two
Bible word search puzzle: In the beginning
Worksheet: I use water to…
Worksheet: Day and night
Coloring page: In the beginning…

 Closing prayer:
End the lesson with a small prayer.

Trace the Words

Color the pictures.

✦ Day One ✦

On day One, God created the night and the day.
Write the number 1. Color the picture.

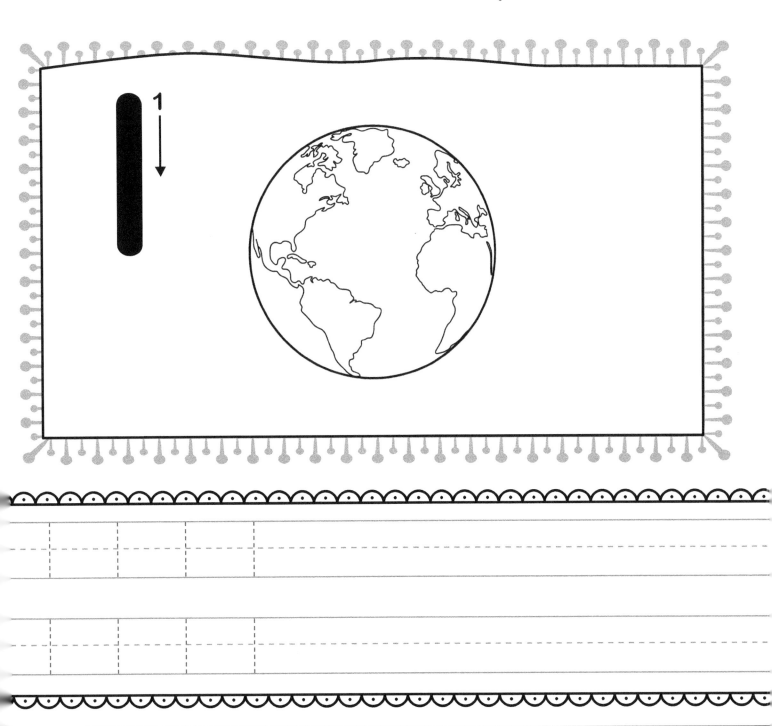

✴ Day Two ✴

On day Two, God created water and sky.
Write the number 2. Color the pictures.

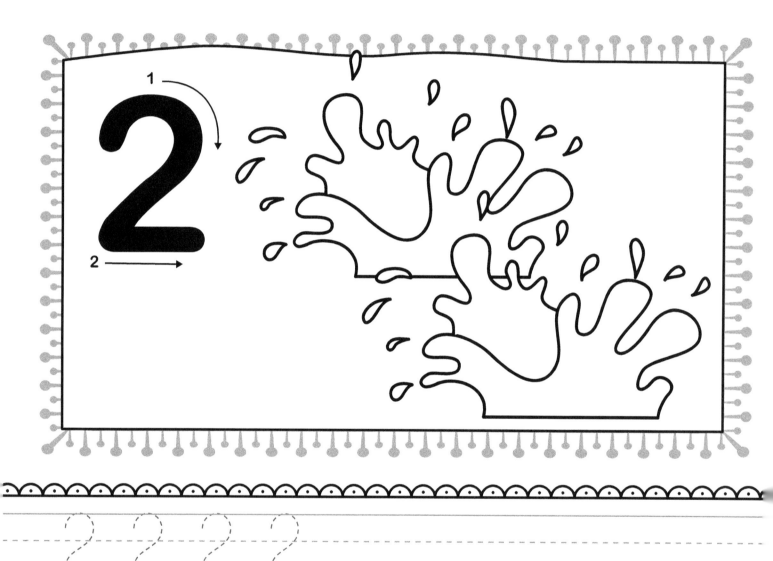

🌿 Match the pictures 🌿

Draw a line to match the pictures with the sentences.
Color the pictures.

 I see
day.

 I see
night.

 I see
water.

I see
sky.

🌿 Day One 🌿

Parents: Read Genesis 1:5 with your child.
Color the picture.

"God named the light 'day' and the darkness 'night.'"

🍃 Day Two 🍃

Parents: Read Genesis 1:6 with your child.
Color the picture.

"Let there be sky and water."

🌿 In the beginning 🌿

Find and circle each of the words from the list below.

```
S X G L D E
K Z D S A A
Y Q X R Y R
B T G O D T
N I G H T H
W A T E R D
```

DAY   NIGHT
WATER   SKY
EARTH   GOD

🌿 I use water to... 🌿

God created water for you to use.
Color the items that use water in your home.

🌿 Day and night 🌿

Parents, ask your children: What do you do during the daytime? What do you do at nighttime?
Color the sun and moon.

"In the beginning, GOD created the heavens and earth."

(Genesis 1:1)

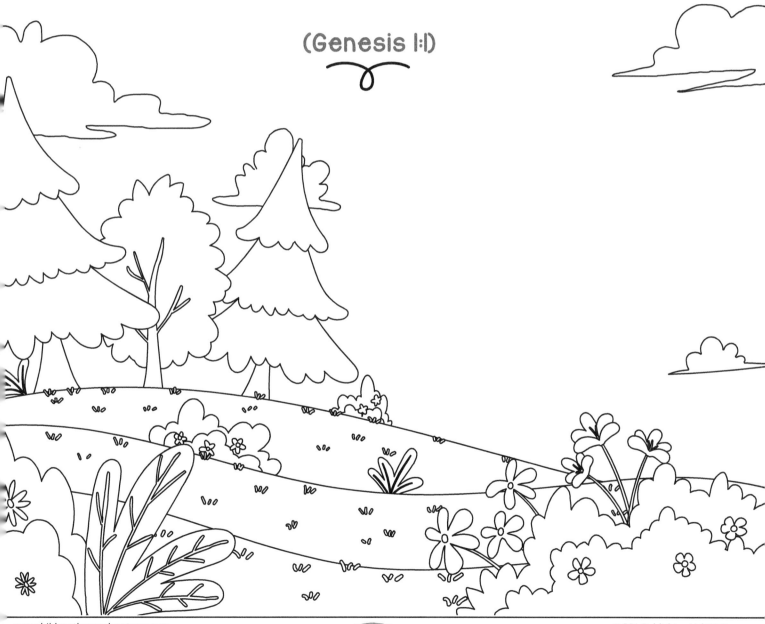

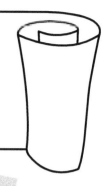

LESSON 2 | Lesson Plan
Dry land and plants

Teacher: _____

Today's Bible passage: Genesis 1:9-13

Welcome prayer:
Pray a simple prayer with the children before you begin the lesson.

Lesson objectives:
In this lesson, children will learn:
1. What God created on the third day
2. What type of plants grew from the earth

Did You Know?
Every plant made its own kind of seeds.

Bible lesson overview:
God said, "Let the water under the sky be gathered together so dry land will appear." He named the land "earth," and the water "seas." Then God said, "Let the earth grow grass, plants that make grain, and fruit trees. The fruit trees will make fruit with seed in it. Let these plants grow on the earth." The earth grew grass and plants that made grain. And it grew trees that made fruit with seeds in it. Every plant made its own kind of seeds. There was evening and then there was morning. This was the third day.

Let's Review:
Questions to ask your students:
1. What did God name the land?
2. What did God name the water?
3. What did the earth grow?
4. What did every plant make?
5. What did God create on Day Three?

 A memory verse to help children remember God's Word:
"The earth grew grass and plants that made grain." (Genesis 1:12)

Activities:
Worksheet: W is for water
Bible puzzle: What did God call 'dry land'?
Numbers worksheet: Day three
Connect the dots: Plants and flowers
Bible activity: God created land
Bible craft: Make a tree!
Worksheet: Trace the Words
Worksheet: What's different?
Worksheet: How do plants grow?
Worksheet: Day three
Worksheet: God made fruit
Alphabet worksheets: S is for seed

 Closing prayer:
End the lesson with a small prayer.

★ W is for water ★

is for

water

What did God call 'dry land'?

Fill in the blanks using the chart below.

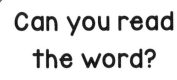

Can you read the word?

$$\overline{\quad} \; \overline{\quad} \; \overline{\quad} \; \overline{\quad} \; \overline{\quad}$$

5   1   18   20   8

A	B	C	D	E	F	G	H	I	J	K	L	M
1	2	3	4	5	6	7	8	9	10	11	12	13
N	O	P	Q	R	S	T	U	V	W	X	Y	Z
14	15	16	17	18	19	20	21	22	23	24	25	26

✷ Day Three ✷

On day Three, God created land and sea, plants and trees.
Write the number 3. Color the pictures.

Plants and flowers

On day Three, God created plants and flowers.
Connect the dots to see the picture.

🌿 Trace the Words 🌿

Color the pictures.

🍃 What's different? 🍃

Circle the picture that is different.

"The earth grew grass and plants made grain."

God made fruit

God made trees that grow fruit. Trace the word fruit.
Can you name the fruit below?

🌿 S is for Seed 🌿

God gave us seeds to grow food (Genesis 1:29).
Trace the letters. Color the picture.

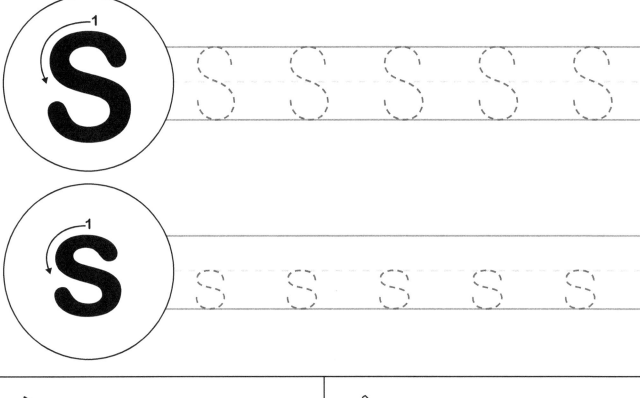

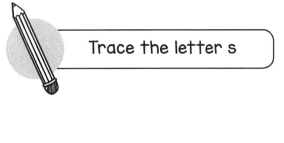

Trace the letter s

Color the seed

s e e d

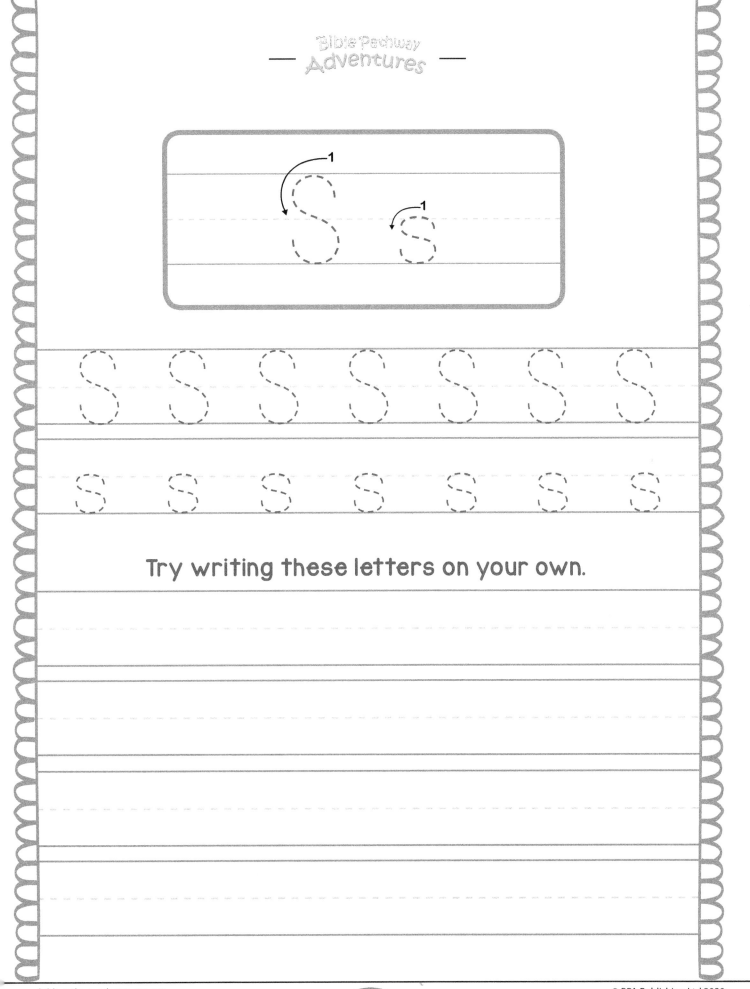

Try writing these letters on your own.

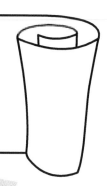

LESSON 3 | Lesson Plan
Sun, moon, and stars

_____

Teacher: _____

Today's Bible passage: Genesis 1:14-19

Welcome prayer:
Pray a simple prayer with the children before you begin the lesson.

Lesson objectives:
In this lesson, children will learn:
1. The purpose of lights in the sky
2. Which two lights rule the day and the night

Did You Know?
The sun is a bigger than the moon.

Bible lesson overview:
God said, "Let there be lights in the sky. These lights will separate the day from the night. They will be used to show signs and seasons (Appointed Times), and to show days and years. They will be in the sky to shine light on the earth." He made two large lights. He made the larger light to rule the day (sun) and the smaller light to rule the night (moon). He also made the stars. God put the moon and the stars in the sky to shine on the earth. There was evening and then there was morning. This was the fourth day.

Let's Review:

Questions to ask your students:

1. Why did God put two lights in the sky?
2. What is the name of the larger light?
3. What is the name of the smaller light?
4. What did God create on Day Four?
5. God made the sun, moon, and _____?

 A memory verse to help children remember God's Word:

"God made two large lights in the sky." (Genesis 1:16)

Activities:

Worksheet: Color me!
Numbers worksheet: Day four
Coloring page: The heavens
Worksheet: Sun, moon, and stars
Worksheet: What gives light?
Coloring page: Sun, moon, stars
Bible flashcards
Worksheet: Complete the pattern
Bible craft: God's creation
Coloring page: Day four
Worksheet: What is opposite?
Worksheet: The number four
Worksheet: Days of the week

 Closing prayer:

End the lesson with a small prayer.

🌿 Color me! 🌿

Color the things God made on Day Three green.
Color the things God made on Day Four blue.

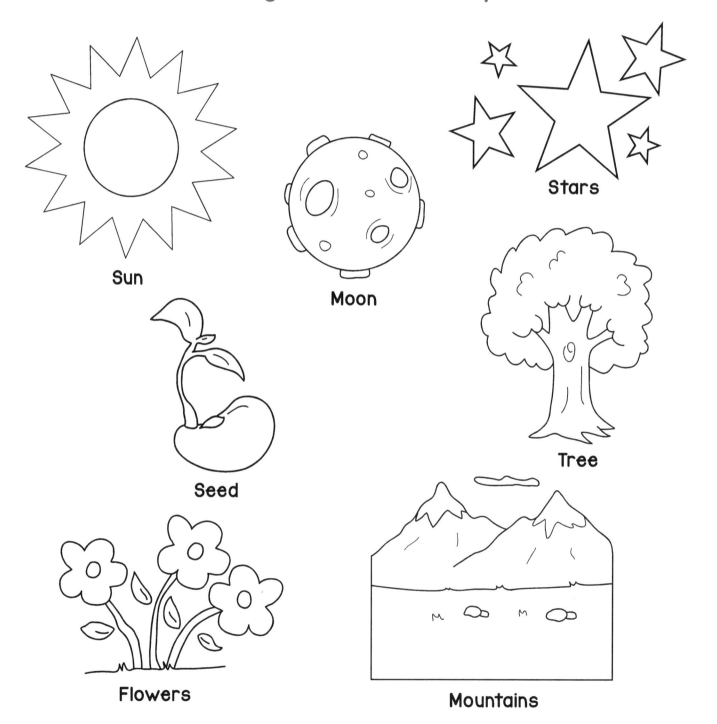

Sun

Moon

Stars

Seed

Tree

Flowers

Mountains

✶ Day Four ✶

On day Four, God made the sun, moon, and stars.
Write the number 4. Color the pictures.

"The heavens declare the glory of God. "

(Psalm 19:1)

🌿 Sun Moon Stars 🌿

Trace the sun, moon, and star. Color the pictures.

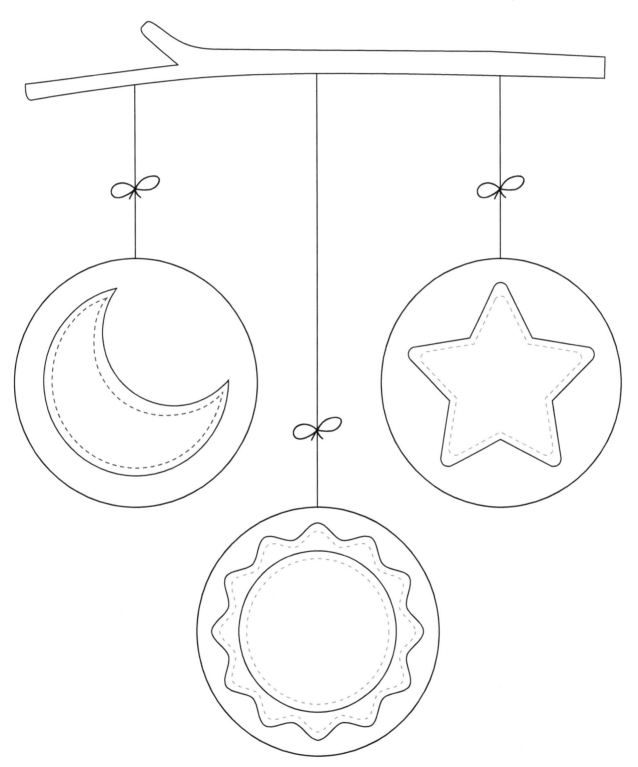

🌿 What gives light? 🌿

God created two lights in the sky; the moon and the sun.
Color the items that give light.

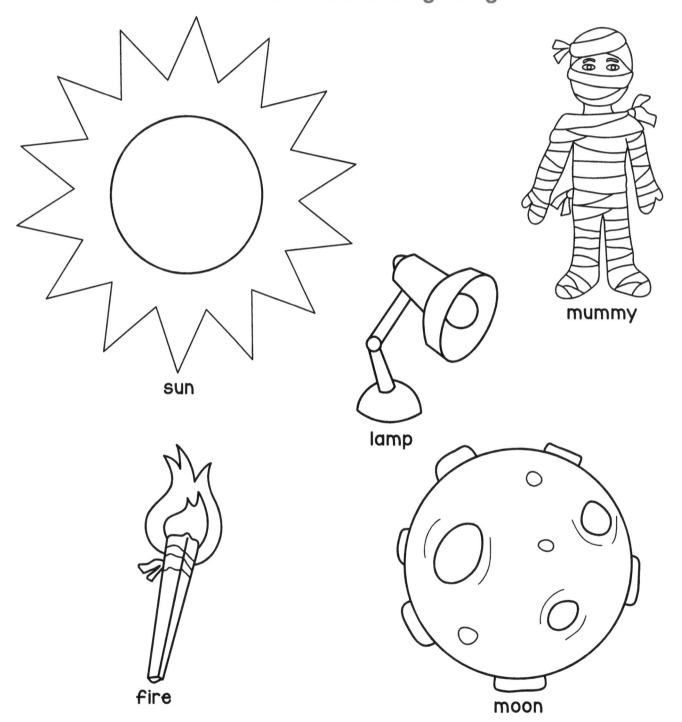

sun

lamp

mummy

fire

moon

🍃 Sun, moon and stars 🍃

God created the sun, moon, and stars.
Color the pictures.

"Let there be lights in the sky."

🍃 What is opposite? 🍃

The sun is big and the moon is small.
Draw a line to match each item with its opposite.
Color the opposite items the same way.

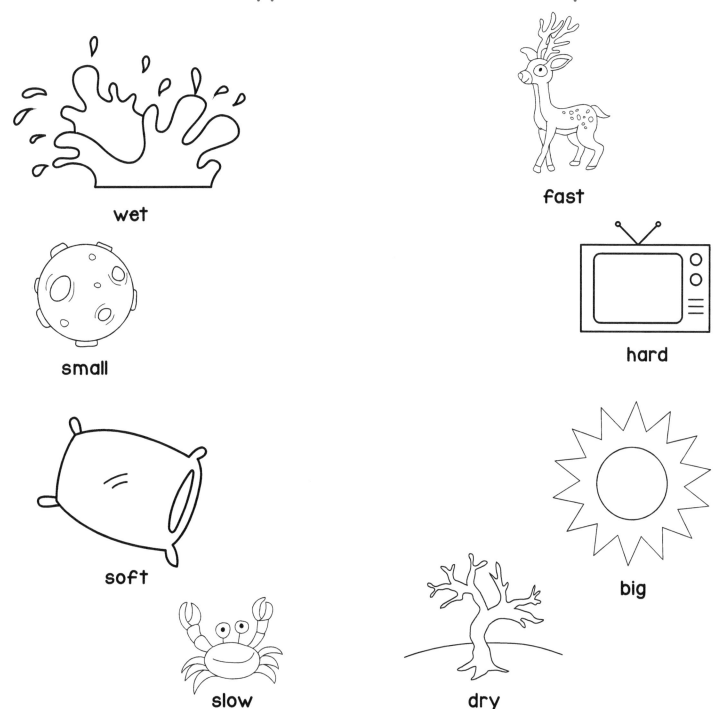

wet

fast

small

hard

soft

big

slow

dry

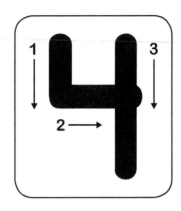 

On Day Four, God said, "Let there be lights in the heavens…" (Genesis 1:14) Trace the number 4.

Write the number four in the boxes below.

How many fingers are there?

What did God create on Day Four?

Days of the Week

God created lights in the sky.
These show us the days of the week.
Fill in the letters to write the days of the week.

SUN D A Y   THURS __ __ __

MON __ __ __   FRI __ __ __

TUE __ __ __   SATUR __ __ __

WEDNES __ __ __

LESSON 4 | Lesson Plan
Birds and sea animals

Teacher: _____

Today's Bible passage: Genesis 1:20-23

Welcome prayer:
Pray a simple prayer with the children before you begin the lesson.

Lesson objectives:
In this lesson, children will learn:
1. What God created to fill the sea
2. What God created to fill the sky

Did You Know?
Most of the earth's water is in the sea.

Bible lesson overview:
God said, "Let the water be filled with many living things. Let there be birds to fly in the air." Then God created the large sea animals. He created many living things in the sea and lots of bird to fly in the air. He blessed the living things in the sea and told them to have babies and fill the seas. And He blessed the birds in the sky and told them to have lots of babies. There was evening and then there was morning. This was the fifth day.

Let's Review:

Questions to ask your students:

1. What did God create to fill the sea?
2. What did God create to fly in the sky?
3. What did God tell the sea animals to do?
4. What did God tell the birds to do?
5. On which day did God create the birds and the sea animals?

 A memory verse to help children remember God's Word:

"God saw that it was good." (Genesis 1:21)

 Activities:

Worksheet: Birds and fish
Worksheet: Day five
Worksheet: Parts of a bird
Worksheet: Parts of a fish
Bible craft: Make a fish!
Worksheet: What flies and what swims?
Worksheet: I spy sea animals!
Worksheet: Circle the birds
Coloring page: Day five
Worksheet: What's the Word?
Bible activity: God created birds

 Closing prayer:
End the lesson with a small prayer.

🌿 Birds and Fish 🌿

On Day Five, God made the birds and fish.
Trace the words. Color the pictures.

birds

fish

✷ Day Five ✷

On day Five, God made the sea animals and birds.
Write the number 5. Color the pictures.

🌿 Parts of a bird 🌿

On day Five, God created birds.
Can you name the parts of a bird?

head   eye   wing

beak   foot

🌿 Parts of a fish 🌿

On day Five, God created fish and sea animals.
Can you name the parts of a fish?

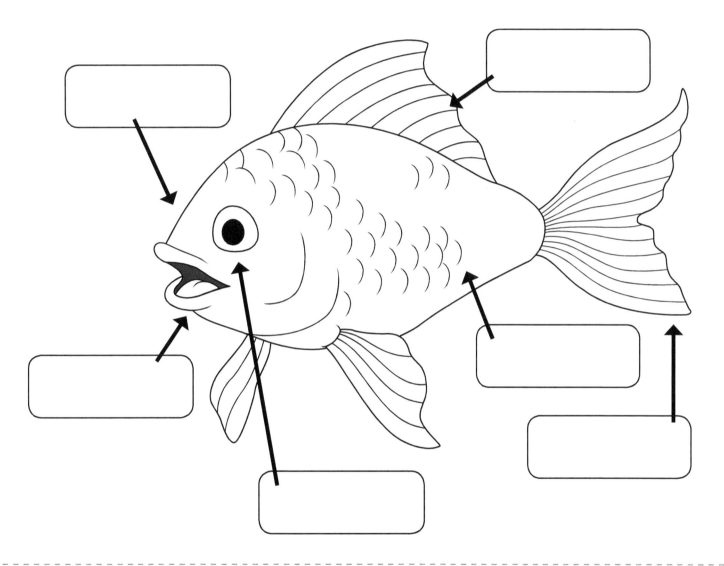

head	eye	mouth
tail	fin	scales

🌿 Make a fish! 🌿

You will need:
1. Paper plates
2. Paint, felt pens, or crayons
3. Scissors and stapler (adults only)
4. Extra-strength glue sticks or school glue
5. Glitter, tissue paper, craft eyes, foil, sequins, etc

Instructions:

1. Cut out a triangle shape from the paper plate. Staple or glue it to the opposite side of the plate to create a tail.
2. Help your child to color their fish with paint or crayons.
3. Decorate your fish with craft eyes, glitter, tissue paper, sequins, etc.

ta-da!

What flies and what swims?

Color the animals that can fly.

🌿 I spy sea animals! 🌿

Color the same sea animal a single color.
Then count each animal and write the number on the label.

🍃 Circle the birds 🍃

Trace the word 'bird'. Circle the birds below.
Color the birds.

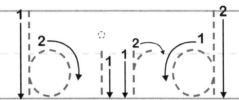

"God created the fish and the birds."

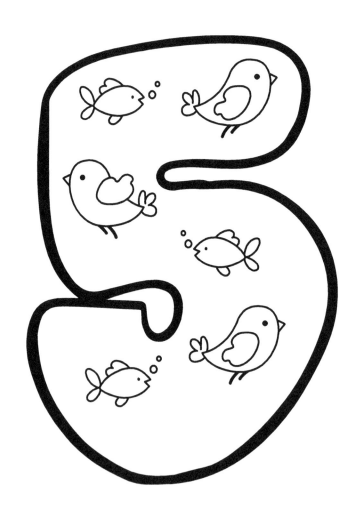

🌿 What's the Word? 🌿

Read the word. Draw a line to the picture it matches with.

1. bird

2. fish

3. sun

4. seed

| LESSON 5 | # Lesson Plan
Animals, man, and the Sabbath |

Teacher: _____

Today's Bible passage: Genesis 1:24-2:3

Welcome prayer:
Pray a simple prayer with the children before you begin the lesson.

Lesson objectives:
In this lesson, children will learn:
1. What God created on the sixth day
2. Why God created the Sabbath

Did You Know?
God made the Sabbath day so we can rest.

Bible lesson overview:
God made every kind of animal. He made the wild animals, the tame animals, and all the small crawling things. Then He said, "Let's make people. They will rule over the fish in the sea and the birds in the air, and all the animals." He created a male and female that were like Himself. He gave them plants and fruit trees for food. And He gave the animals green plants to eat. This was the sixth day. On the seventh day God rested from His work. He made the seventh day a holy day (Sabbath). He made it special because on that day He rested from all the work He did while creating the world.

Let's Review:
Questions to ask your students:
1. God created what kind of animals?
2. What kind of people did God create?
3. What did God give the people to eat?
4. What did God give the animals to eat?
5. What did God do on the seventh day?

 A memory verse to help children remember God's Word:
"God blessed the Sabbath and made it holy." (Genesis 2:3)

 ## Activities:
Worksheet: What a lot of animals
Worksheet: Day six
Coloring page: God created man
Coloring page: God created a woman
Alphabet worksheets: A is for Adam
Worksheet: Big & small
Coloring page: Day six
Bible activity: Days of creation
Bible word search puzzle: The creation
Worksheet: The Sabbath
Coloring page: Draw what you do on the Sabbath
Coloring page: The Sabbath
Certificate of Award

 ## Closing prayer:
End the lesson with a small prayer.

🍃 What a lot of animals! 🍃

Can you count them all? Write the number in the box.

monkey

elephant

buffalo

deer

hippo

moose

donkey

rabbit

Day Six

On day Six, God made people and animals.
Write the number 6. Color the pictures.

 God created a man

On day Six, God created a man.
Trace the word. Color the picture.

man

God created a woman

On day Six, God created a woman.
Trace the word. Connect the dots to see the picture.

woman

A is for Adam

The first man was called Adam (Genesis 2:20).
Trace the letters. Color the picture.

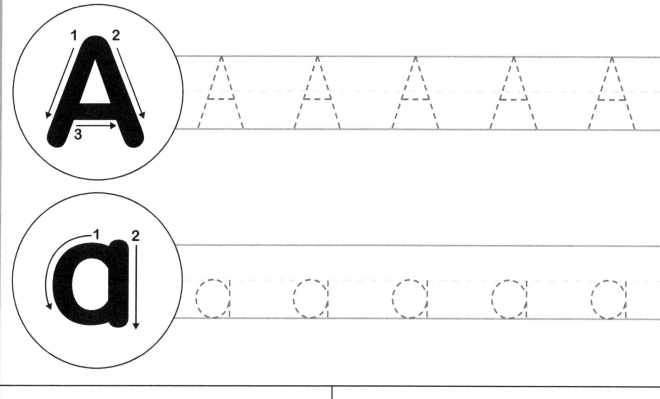

Trace the letter a

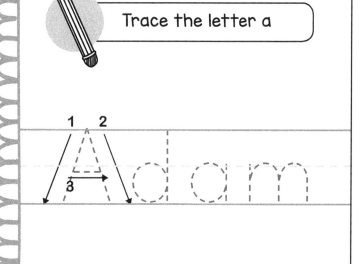

Color Adam

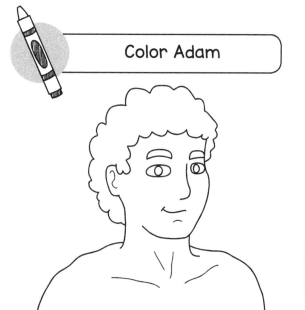

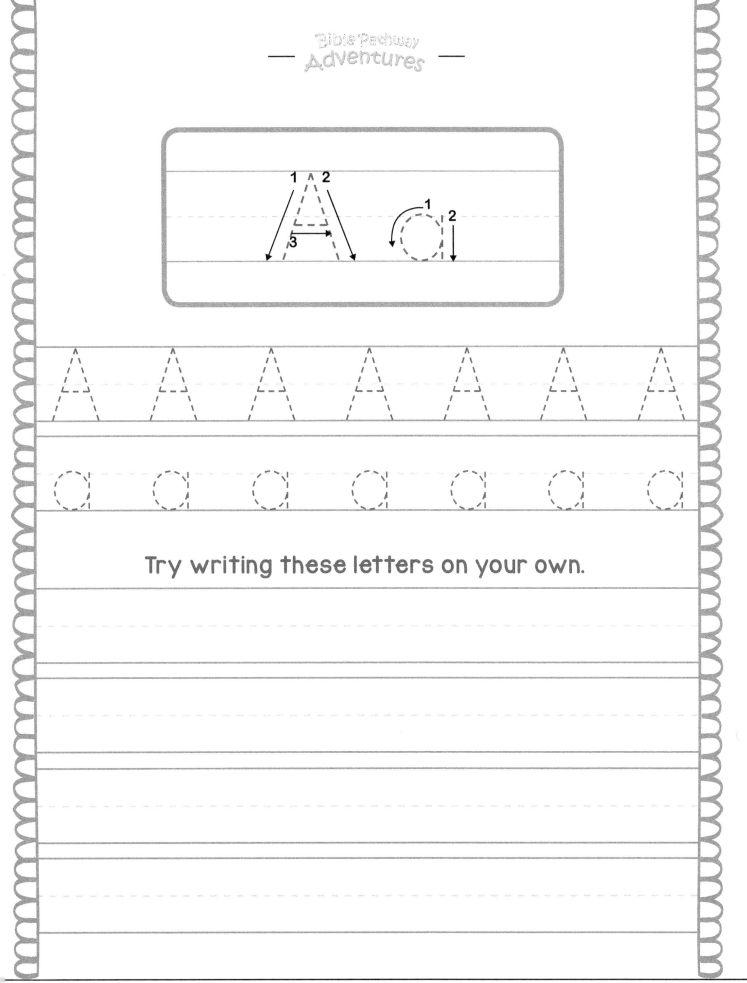

Try writing these letters on your own.

🌿 Big & small 🌿

God created seeds that grow into trees (Genesis 1:29).
A seed is small. A tree is big.

big

small

Draw something big. | Draw something small.

"God made every kind of animal."

🍃 The creation 🍃

Find and circle each of the words from the list below.

```
M T K Y F P
A R Y W I L
N E G V S A
F E D D H N
B I R D S T
S E E D N Z
```

MAN   SEED
PLANT   BIRDS
TREE   FISH

Seven

God rested on the seventh day. He blessed this day and made it holy (Genesis 2:3).

Write the number seven in the boxes below.

How many fingers are there?

What do you do on the Sabbath?

....

The Sabbath

God's people rest on the seventh day.
Draw what you do on the Sabbath.

Remember the Sabbath

Keep it Holy

CRAFTS & PROJECTS

🌿 Day and night 🌿

Compare the day sky and night sky.
Where do the pictures belong? Color and cut out the pictures.
Glue them into the correct section.

Day Sky

Night Sky

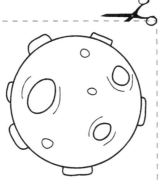

Water and Sky

On day Two, God created water and sky.

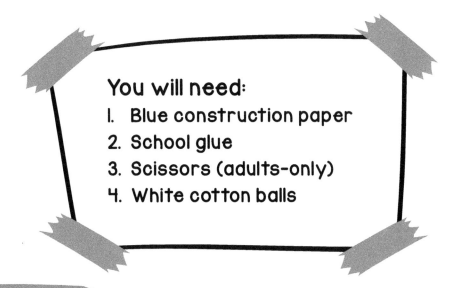

You will need:
1. Blue construction paper
2. School glue
3. Scissors (adults-only)
4. White cotton balls

Instructions:

1. Pull apart the white cotton balls and glue them onto the top half of the blue construction paper
2. Color and cut out the wave template on the next page.
3. Glue the waves onto the bottom half of the blue construction paper.

1.   2.   3.

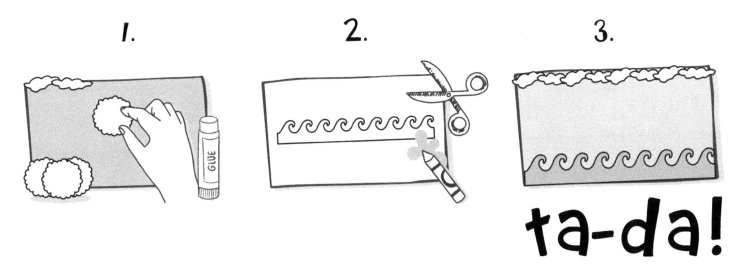

ta-da!

Make a rain cloud

You will need:
1. White and blue card stock
2. Cotton balls and paper plate
3. Yellow paint or crayons
4. School glue, glue stick, and clear tape
5. Scissors (adults only)
6. String or yarn

Instructions:

1. Paste or copy the cloud and raindrop template sheets onto white and blue card stock. Cut out the cloud and raindrops.
2. Glue or tape four pieces of string onto the back of the cloud. Tape three blue raindrops onto each piece of string.
3. Color the paper plate yellow. When the plate is dry, cut out the sun rays. Cut the bottom sun rays from the sun to make it easier to glue the sun to the cloud.
4. Glue the sun to the cloud. Cover the cloud in glue and add cotton balls to make your cloud fluffy.

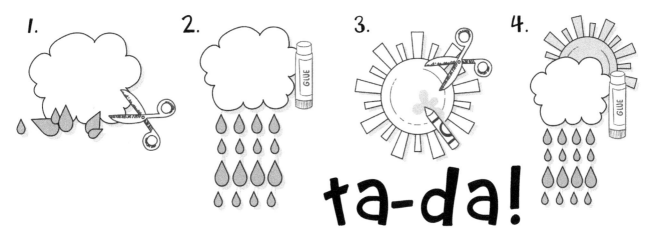

ta-da!

God created land

On day Three, God created land and plants.
Color and cut out the objects. Paste them onto the land.

🍃 Make a tree! 🍃

On Day Three, God made trees. Color the tree and leaves.
Cut out and paste together onto construction paper.

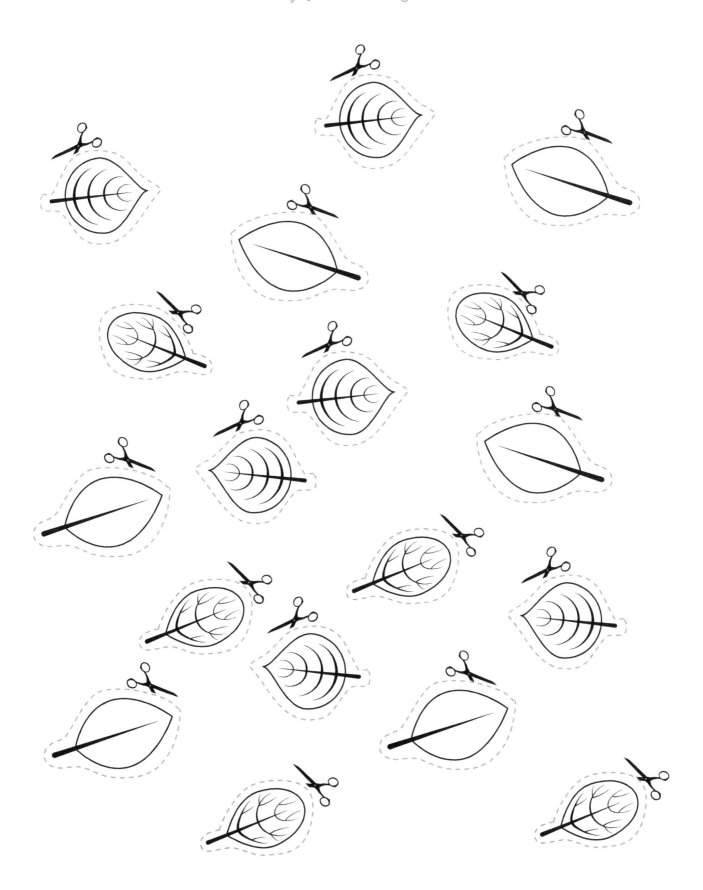

🌱 How do plants grow? 🌱

Color and cut out the different stages of the plant life cycle.
Paste them onto the page in the correct order.

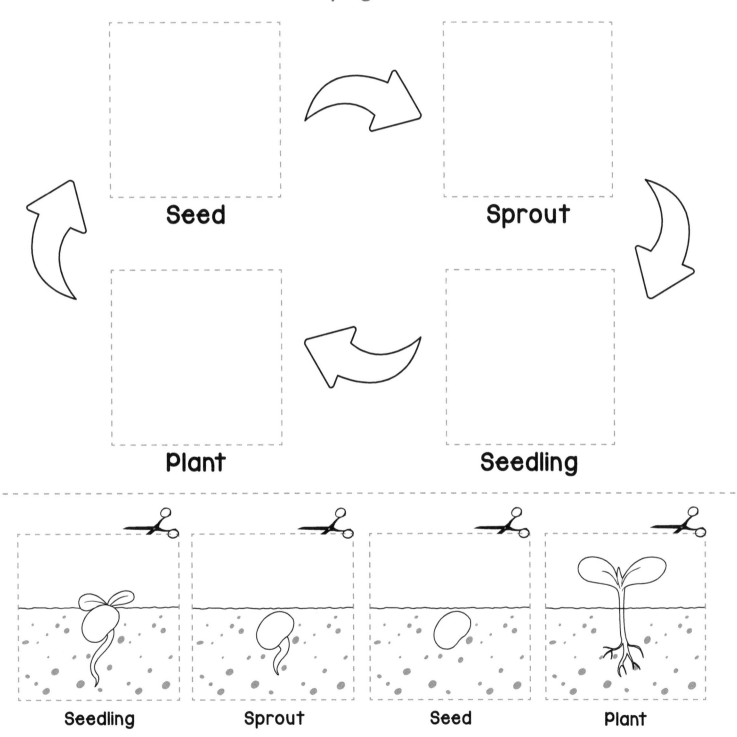

Seed

Sprout

Plant

Seedling

Seedling   Sprout   Seed   Plant

🌿 Flashcards 🌿

Color and cut out the flashcards.
Tape them around your home or classroom!

flower

5

fish

6

fruit

7

animals

8

water

9

grain

10

birds

11

plant

12

🌿 Complete the pattern 🌿

Cut out the objects and place them in the correct box.

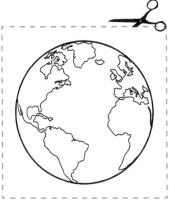

www.biblepathwayadventures.com
The Creation Activity Book (Beginners)

God's creation

You will need:
1. Paint, felt pens, or crayons
2. Card stock
3. Scissors (adult only)
4. School glue or glue sticks

Instructions:

1. Print or copy the circle and sun, moon, and stars templates. Print or paste the circle onto card stock.
2. Cut out the circle. Color half of the circle black, and the other half blue.
3. Color the sun, moon, and stars template. Cut out the sun, moon, and stars, and paste them onto the correct half of the circle.

1.
2.
3.

ta-da!

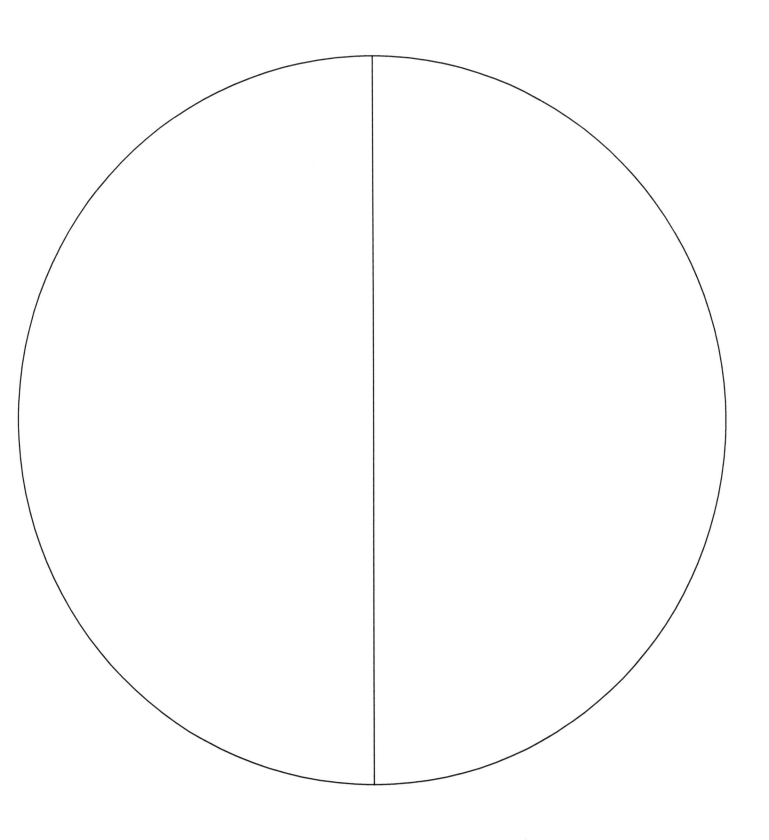

🌿 God created birds 🌿

God created lots of birds. Color and cut out the birds.
Paste them onto the land.

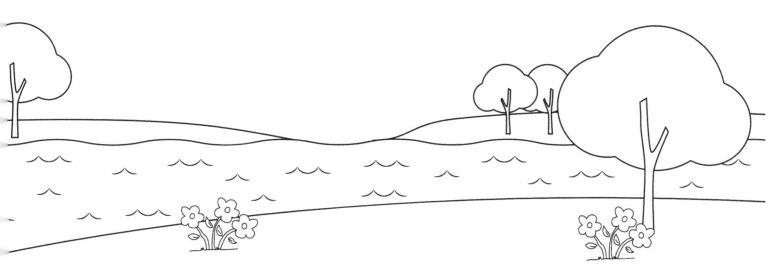

| Duck | Dove | Peacock | Chicken |

🌿 Days of Creation 🌿

Color and cut out the pictures.
Paste them onto the day that God created them.

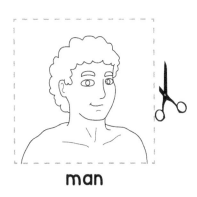

man

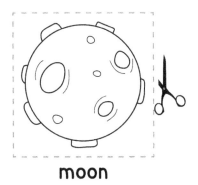

moon

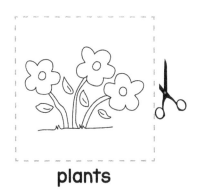

plants

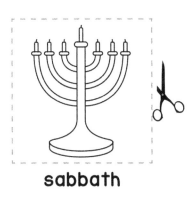

sabbath

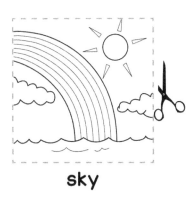

sky

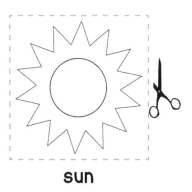

sun

trees

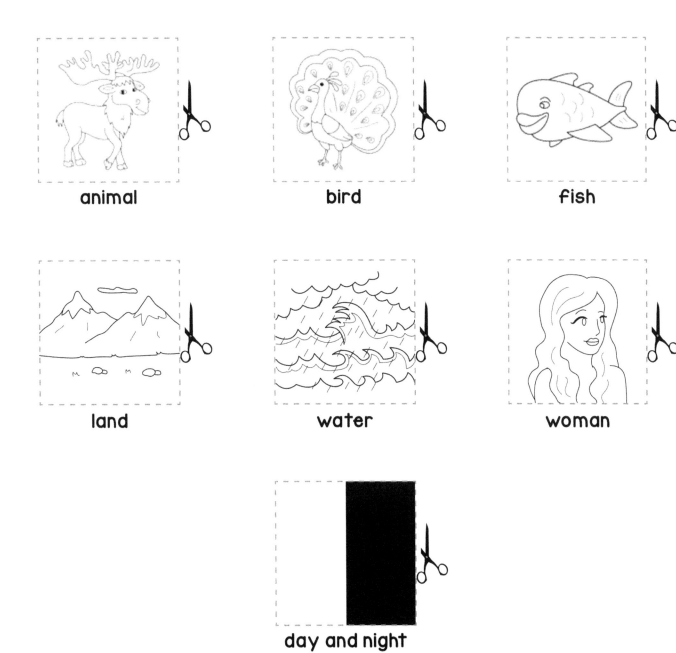

animal

bird

fish

land

water

woman

day and night

Day 1

Day 2

Day 3

Day 4

Day 5

Day 6

Day 7

The Creation

Certificate of Award

Certificate of Award

Congratulations

....

For

....

....
Signed

ANSWER KEY

LESSON ONE: Day & night, water & sky
Let's Review answers:
1. The earth
2. Day
3. Night
4. Two
5. Sky

LESSON TWO: Dry land and plants
Let's Review answers:
1. Earth
2. Sea
3. Grass, grain, and fruit trees
4. Every plant made its own seeds
5. Grass and plants, and fruit trees

LESSON THREE: Sun, moon, and stars
Let's Review answers:
1. To rule the earth, for signs and seasons, days and years
2. Sun
3. Moon
4. Sun, moon, and stars
5. Stars

LESSON FOUR: Birds and sea animals
Let's Review answers:
1. Sea animals
2. Birds
3. Have lots of babies and fill the waters
4. Have lots of babies and fill the sky
5. Day five

LESSON FIVE: Animals, man, and the Sabbath
Let's Review answers:
1. Wild animals, the tame animals, and all the small crawling things
2. Male and female humans
3. Grain bearing plants and fruit trees
4. Green plants
5. God rested on the seventh day

Discover more Activity Books!

Available for purchase at www.biblepathwayadventures.com

INSTANT DOWNLOAD!

Daniel and the Lions	The Creation
Balaam's Donkey	Moses Ten Plagues
Birth of the King	The Exodus
The Story of Joseph	The Story of Esther